PRINT'S BEST T-SHIRT PROMOTIONS

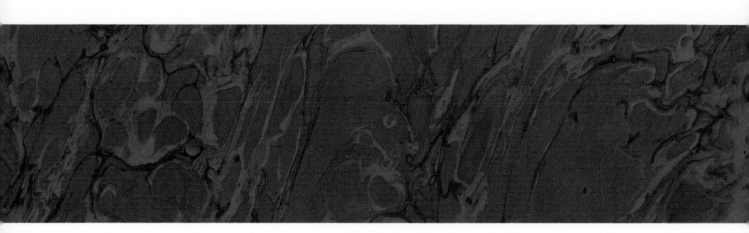

PRINT'S BEST T-SHIRT PROMOTIONS

Library of Congress Catalog Card Number 92-081124
ISBN 0-915734-80-X

RC PUBLICATIONS

President and Publisher: Howard Cadel
Vice President and Editor: Martin Fox
Creative Director: Andrew Kner
Managing Director, Book Projects: Linda Silver
Administrative Assistants: Nancy Silver, Tod Lippy
Assistant Art Director: Nell Coyle

Print's Best
T-SHIRT PROMOTIONS
WINNING DESIGNS FROM PRINT MAGAZINE'S NATIONAL COMPETITION

Edited by

LINDA SILVER

Introduction by

TOM GOSS

Designed by

ANDREW KNER

Published by

RC PUBLICATIONS, INC.
NEW YORK, NY

In the course of compiling their Regional Design Annual, the editors and art director of PRINT often notice particular trends in the practice and application of graphic design. Occasionally, they perceive the introduction of what they consider a new medium for the designer's art. T-shirts, the subject of this book, are just such an example. "When we first started publishing the Regional," recalls PRINT art director, Andrew Kner, "we'd get an occasional T-shirt and say, 'Well, that's kind of neat, let's run it.' Now, not having a T-shirt in an identity program is rare."

It doesn't take too much thought to puzzle out just why T-shirts have grown from being considered a poor medium for graphic design to an almost essential one. All one has to do is walk down a street in any urban center in the world to see what a ubiquitous promotional vehicle they have become. Mail 100 potential clients a promotional brochure and perhaps 200 people will see it. But mail out 100 T-shirts, and assuming they're at all decent looking, you launch 100 walking billboards.

Obviously, their popularity as promotional items lies in the fact that T-shirts are items of clothing—and free ones at that. Most people are loath to simply throw away a new piece of clothing and will at the very least give a T-shirt to someone else if they themselves don't want it. Perhaps a more powerful factor in this than parsimony, however, is fashion. The trend over the past several decades has been to embrace more casual forms of clothing (though not necessarily less costly or less stylish). Brand awareness has been a part of this trend—to such an extent that people want, or are at least willing to flaunt, the name of the brand or designer of their shoes, jeans, and luggage on the items in question. In short, clothing manufacturers have made their products promotional vehicles for themselves, and promotional T-shirts have taken this concept one step further by being clothing that promotes other products and services. As with Gucci, Nike, or Calvin Klein, these products or services must be promoted in a way with which the wearer is willing to be identified—whether through a sense of esthetics, humor, social responsibility, or irreverence, or through loyalty to a restaurant, watering hole, cultural institution, or charity. People seem willing to wear someone else's message because they feel it says something about themselves—which is the essence of fashion.

In terms of T-shirt design itself, it has evolved from straightforward application of a symbol or logo to approaches

CONTENTS

that treat the shirt as a canvas. Whereas designers once simply applied graphics to the front of the shirt, designs now appear on the front and back, wrap around, and are even on the sleeves. "One of the hardest things to get used to when working with T-shirts is that you're printing on a piece of clothing," observes Randy Hamar, a graphic designer with Nike's Air Jordan division. "That means you're printing on fabric with seams. You can't get the kind of fine detail you can in printing on paper. The best you can hope for is the equivalent of a 65-line screen." The reason is that the fabric absorbs the ink and the colors spread through the fibers—the fabric equivalent of dot gain. With T-shirts, however, the color is laid down in areas with a silk-screening process which "flashes," or cures, up to four areas of color, one at a time. "Some people try to get more than four colors by laying down two areas before flashing," Hamar says. "But there are certain color combinations you have to worry about. If, for example, you put yellow and blue down next to one another, you could get a nice line of green in your design." Another issue is that of the "hand" or feel of the two kinds of inks: Water-based inks have a nicer feel to them, but are difficult to work with as they often clog the screens. Oil-based inks are heavier to the touch, but are easier to work with as they don't set until they're flashed. There's also the question of the fabric color. "If you want to put a light color on a dark shirt," Hamar says, "you have to lay down a base of white first. And if you use large areas of light color on a dark shirt, you end up making something that feels like a bullet-proof vest." The cost of producing a batch of T-shirts depends on the number being produced, the number of "placements" (graphics on the front is one placement, front and back two placements, etc.), and the type of inks used. Hamar estimates that 1500 T-shirts (a small run), printed in four colors of oil-based ink with a single placement, would cost $20.00 each.

As with the other books in this series, the over 200 designs included here are collected from recent editions of PRINT's Regional Design Annual, in this case, the 1990 and 1991 editions. Where a T-shirt was part of an extended identity program or promotional campaign, we have presented the shirt with other elements in the campaign. We have made no effort to force the shirts or designs into defined categories; rather, we present them in a manner intended to be inspiring and entertaining—an approach appropriate to the spirit of fun T-shirts represent.—*Tom Goss*

When more than one shirt from a series is shown, *indicates which is the 1990 or 1991 Regional Annual winner.*

5

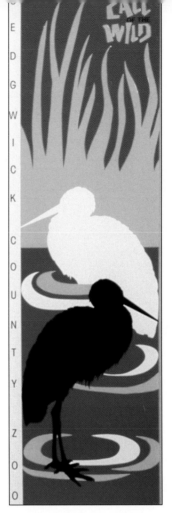

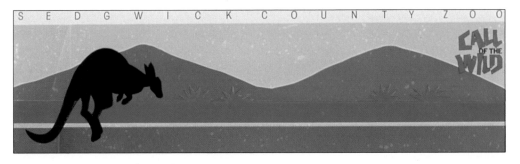

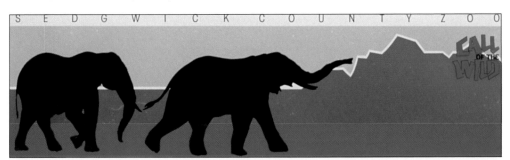

Shirts and posters for a membership campaign.
AGENCY: Lida Advertising, Wichita, Kansas
ART DIRECTOR/ DESIGNER/ ILLUSTRATOR: Cam Woody

DESIGN FIRM:

The Design Group,

Greensboro, North Carolina

DESIGN DIRECTOR:

David R. Gibbs

DESIGNER/ILLUSTRATOR:

Timothy J. Brown

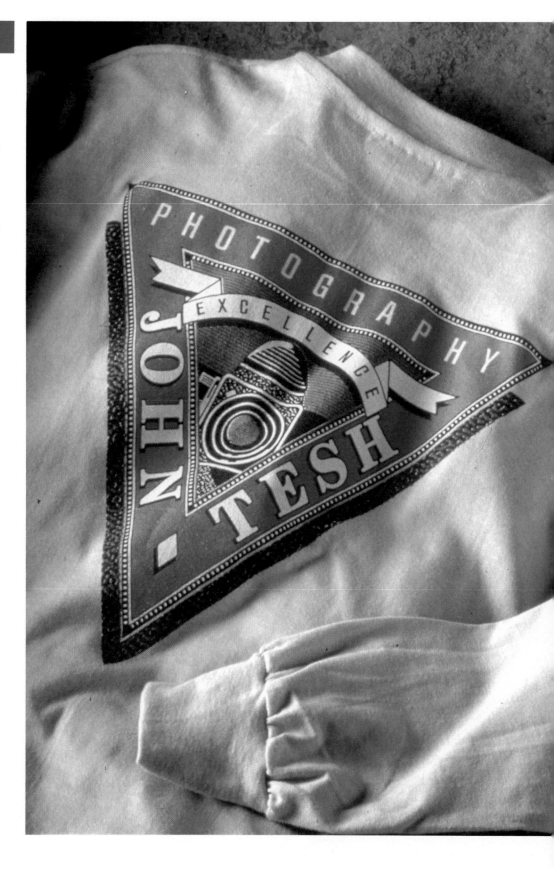

DESIGN FIRM:

Silicon Graphics, Inc.,

Mountain View, California

ART DIRECTOR/DESIGNER/

ILLUSTRATOR:

Frank X. Doyle

LETTERER: Georgia Deaver

DESIGN FIRM:

Watermarks Studio,

Westerly, Rhode Island

ART DIRECTOR/DESIGNER/

ILLUSTRATOR: Suwin Chan

Promotional shirts for
Adobe Extend software,
Adobe Japan, and Adobe
High Tech Games software.
DESIGN FIRM:
Woods+Woods,
San Francisco, California
ART DIRECTOR:
Russell Brown (High Tech
Games)
DESIGNER/ILLUSTRATOR:
Paul Woods

アドビ システムズ ジャパン

World cup soccer promotion (opposite). "Verbage" series (below).

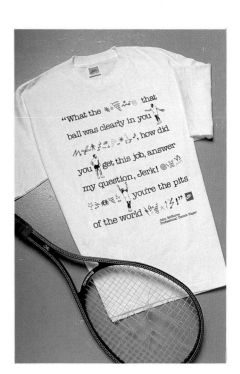

ITALIA

1·9·9·0

World cup soccer promotion

(opposite).

"Stamp" series (below).

DESIGN FIRM:

Nike Apparel, Beaverton,

Oregon

ART DIRECTOR/DESIGNER/

ILLUSTRATOR:

Guido Brouwers

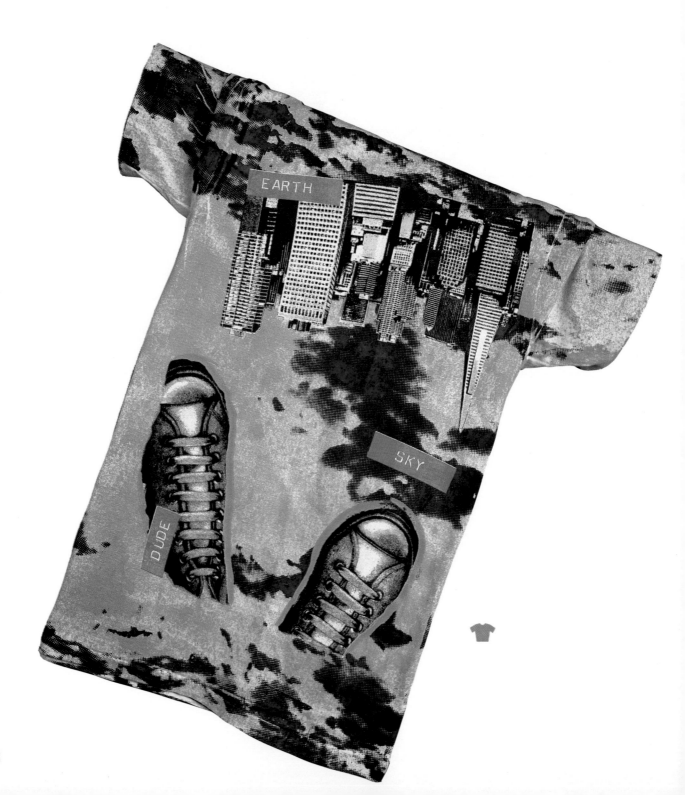

DESIGN FIRM:

Winterland Productions,

San Francisco, California

ART DIRECTOR:

Sandra Horvat Vallely

DESIGNERS/ILLUSTRATORS:

Tim Mitoma (Earth/Sky/

Dude), Raymond Larrett

(NO Where)

Companion—front and

back—to the shirt on

preceding spread (right).

another series (below).

DESIGN FIRM:

Mayeda Art Direction +

Design, San Diego,

California

ART DIRECTOR/DESIGNER:

Scott Mayeda

PRINTER: Dyno Brands

COPYWRITER: UBU

Fish Co. (Restaurant)

DESIGN FIRM:

Rusty Kay & Associates,

Santa Monica, California

ART DIRECTOR: Rusty Kay

DESIGNER/ILLUSTRATOR:

Susan Rogers

DESIGN FIRM:

The Duffy Design Group,

Minneapolis, Minnesota

CREATIVE DIRECTOR:

Joe Duffy

ART DIRECTORS:

Joe Duffy, Haley Johnson

DESIGNERS:

Haley Johnson, Joe Duffy

ILLUSTRATOR:

Lynn Schulte

DESIGN FIRM:

Stephens Design, Santa

Rosa, California

ART DIRECTOR/

DESIGNER/ ILLUSTRATOR/

COPYWRITER:

Dave Stephens

CLIENT: EMG Pickups, Inc.

KUER FM 90

DESIGN FIRM:

Traci O'Very Covey, Salt
Lake City, Utah

ART DIRECTOR/

DESIGNER/ ILLUSTRATOR:

Traci O'Very Covey

DESIGN FIRM:

Stephen Curran Design,

North Miami Beach, Florida

ART DIRECTOR/

DESIGNER: Stephen Curran

Paula P. Bondi
Assistant

PITTSBURGH
FILM · OFFICE
Benedum Trees Building, Suite 1300
Pittsburgh, Pennsylvania 15222
412-261-2744 Fax 412-471-3454

PITTSBURGH
FILM · OFFICE
Benedum Trees Building, Suite 1300
Pittsburgh, Pennsylvania 15222
412-261-2744 Fax 412-471-3454

PITTSBURGH
FILM · OFFICE
Benedum Trees Building, Suite 1300
Pittsburgh, Pennsylvania 15222
412-261-2744 Fax 412-471-3454

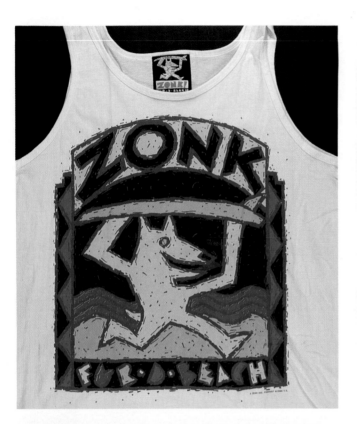

DESIGN FIRM:

Sabin Design, San Diego,

California

ART DIRECTOR: Greg Sabin

DESIGNER/ILLUSTRATOR:

Tracy Sabin

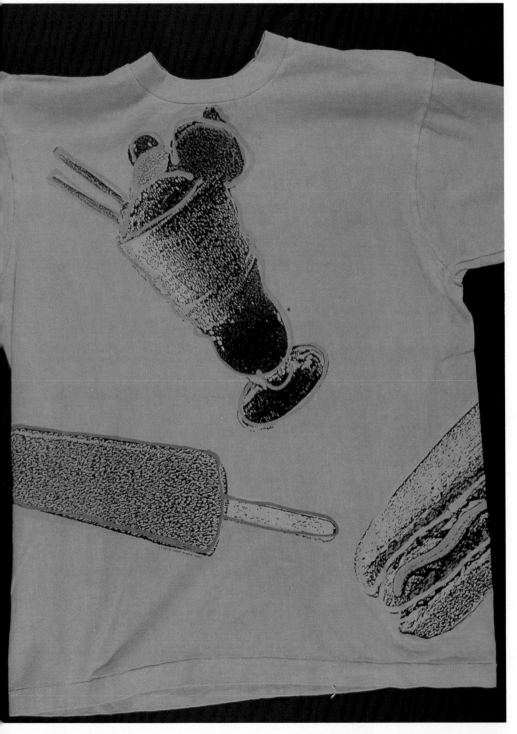

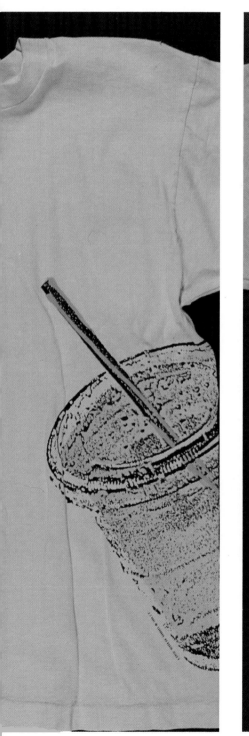

DESIGN FIRM:

Sabin Design, San Diego,

California

ART DIRECTOR:

Richard Sawyer

DESIGNER/ILLUSTRATOR:

Tracy Sabin

Morris Advertising & Design

Front.

AGENCY:

Morris Advertising &

Design, Newport Beach,

California

CREATIVE DIRECTOR:

Anne Morris

ART DIRECTOR/

ILLUSTRATOR: Paul Gyuro

Firstar Corporation (Bank)

DESIGN FIRM:

Hanson Graphic,

Milwaukee, Wisconsin

ART DIRECTOR:

Ken Hanson

DESIGNERS: Kathy Fabry,

Joe Sutter, Marie Claire

Salscheider

ILLUSTRATOR:

Jon Hargreaves

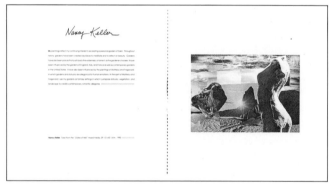

Spreads from catalog for

"Collage" exhibition.

DESIGN FIRM:

Tocquigny Design, Inc.,

Austin, Texas

ART DIRECTOR:

Yvonne Tocquigny

DESIGNER: Scott Herron

ACCOUNT SERVICES:

Sonia Browder

31 ARTISTS MIX IT UP

Jacket (center), pin (opposite page), hat and packs (top) and poster (below).

DESIGN FIRM:

Hornall Anderson Design Works, Seattle, Washington

ART DIRECTOR:

Jack Anderson

DESIGNERS:

Jack Anderson, Jani Drewfs

CLIENT:

Cascade Bicycle Club

DESIGN FIRM:

McCollum Design, Glendale,

California

DESIGNER/ILLUSTRATOR:

Sudi McCollum

Los Gatos Dianetics Center

River City Dog Show

ART DIRECTOR:

Christopher Moroney, San

Antonio, Texas

DESIGNER/ILLUSTRATOR:

Christopher Moroney

PRINTER:

Austin Screen Printing

CLIENT:

Moroney Graphic Arts

A combination restaurant,

deli, wine shop, caterer,

bakery, and art gallery.

DESIGN FIRM:

Hornall Anderson Design

Works, Seattle, Washington

ART DIRECTOR/

DESIGNER:

Jack Anderson

DESIGNER/ILLUSTRATOR:

Julia LaPine

I T A L I A

Delicatessen

Caterers

Art Gallery

Cafe

Seattle

I T A L I A

MCMXC

DESIGN FIRM:

Pecos River Learning

Centers, Santa Fe, New

Mexico

ART DIRECTOR/

DESIGNER: Nancy Glazer

PHOTOGRAPHERS:

Valerie Santagto, Tom

Callanan (Let Go & Grow)

Ninth annual Illinois River trip for clients, associates and friends.

DESIGN FIRM:
Eskridge Designer/Illustrator, Tulsa, Oklahoma
ART DIRECTOR/
DESIGNER: Lynn Eskridge
COPYWRITER: Tom Wirt
SILKSCREEN: Underdog

ROW VS WADE

THE CURRENT EVENT OF 1990

THE ESKRIDGE NINTH ANNUAL

MEMORIAL DAY FLOAT, MAY 27

Killian & Company (Advertising)

DESIGN FIRM:

Killian & Company, Chicago,

Illinois

ART DIRECTOR/

DESIGNER: Bob Killian

(sweatshirt)

DESIGNER: Elissa Scott

(T-shirt)

ILLUSTRATOR:

Michael Kurtz

Shirt was used by CLX to successfully pitch the Roller Blade account.

DESIGN FIRM: CLX, Minneapolis, Minnesota

ART DIRECTOR/ DESIGNER/ ILLUSTRATOR: Peter Winecke

DESIGN FIRM: Modern Dog,

Seattle, Washington

ART DIRECTORS:

Jim Walters, Bill Reichert

DESIGNER/ILLUSTRATOR/

COPYWRITER:

Michael Strassburger

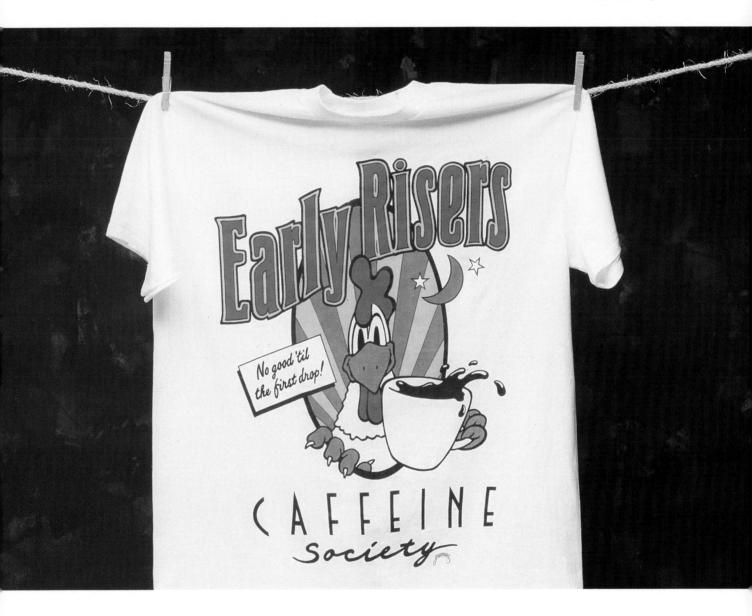

DESIGN FIRM: Modern Dog,

Seattle, Washington

ART DIRECTOR:

Mark Dellplain

DESIGNER:

Michael Strassburger

DESIGN FIRM:

Harborside Graphics,

Belfast, Maine

ART DIRECTOR: Liz Stanley

DESIGNER/ILLUSTRATOR:

Fred Ribeck/Ribeck and Co.

CLIENT:

Harborside Graphics

Sportswear

DESIGNER/ILLUSTRATOR:

Barry Mitchell,

Birmingham, Alabama

CLIENT:

Metro Humane Shelter

Poster and print ad
(below).
DESIGN FIRM:
Sullivan & Sullivan,
Pensacola, Florida
DESIGNER/ILLUSTRATOR:
Jem Sullivan
PRINTER: Ranger Printing

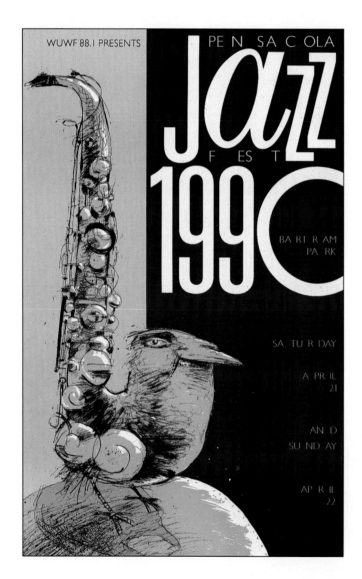

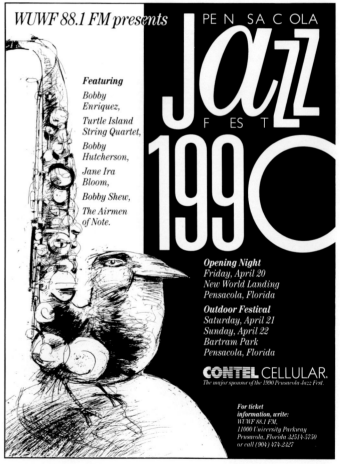

Collection designed for

Bloomingdale's California

promotion.

DESIGN FIRM:

Morla Design, San

Francisco, California

ART DIRECTOR/

DESIGNER/ ILLUSTRATOR:

Jennifer Morla

DESIGN FIRM:

Sese/Paul Designs,

Bethesda, Maryland

ART DIRECTOR/

DESIGNER/ILLUSTRATOR:

Maria A. Sese

CREATIVE DIRECTOR:

Christopher Paul (Moo

River)

GIVE·A·DOG·A·BONE

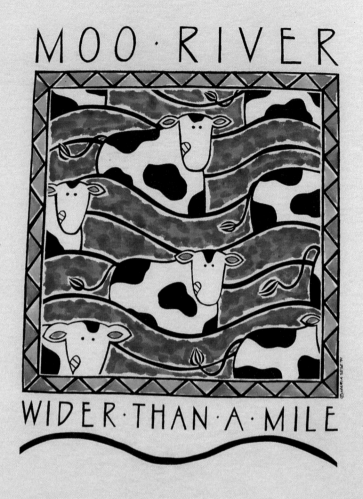

DESIGN FIRM:

Die Brucken Artwear,

Columbus, Ohio

DESIGNERS:

Chip Barthelmes (Lucky

Charms, Hand in Glove,

Swiss Army Clock, Dance),

Kirk Richard Smith

(Skeletons)

ILLUSTRATORS:

Chip Barthelmes (Lucky

Charms, Hand in Glove,

Swiss Army Clock, Dance),

Kirk Richard Smith

(Skeletons)

PRINTER:

Coloract Graphics

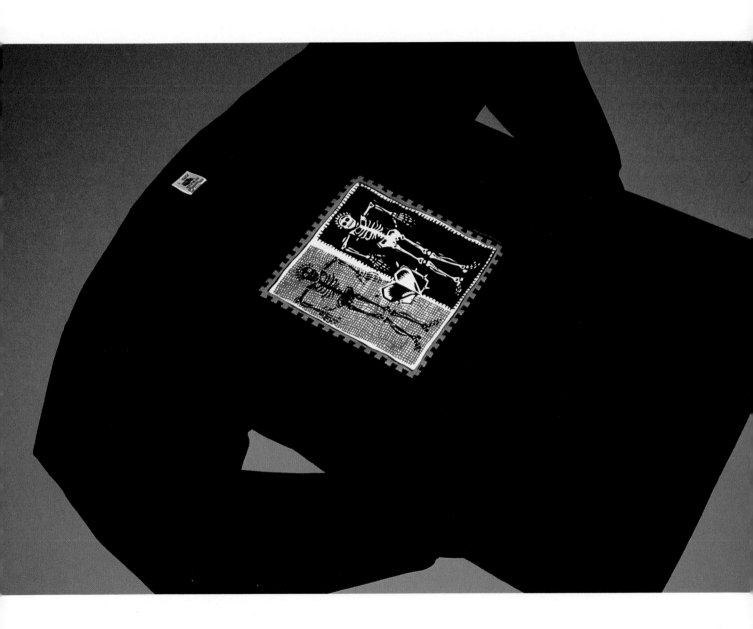

American Demographics (Graphic Design)

DESIGN FIRM:

American Demographics,

Ithaca, New York

DESIGNER: Jim Keller

SCREEN PRINTER:

Screen Graphics

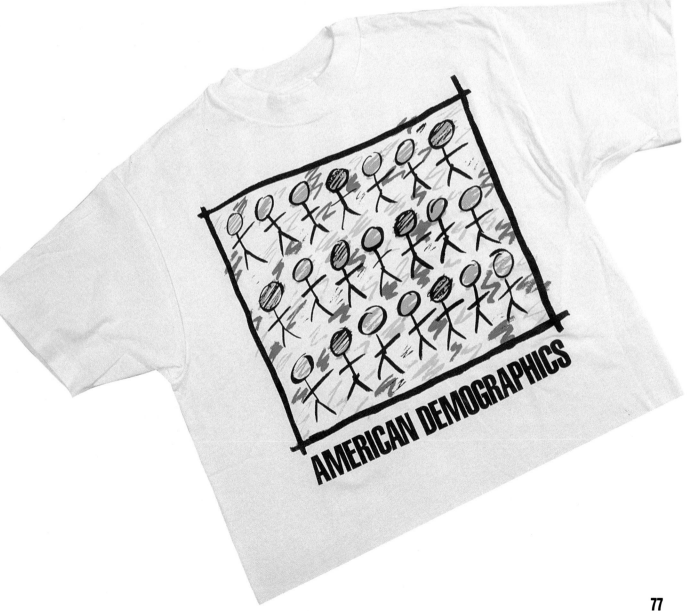

AGENCY: Dally Advertising,

Arlington, Texas

ART DIRECTOR/

DESIGNER/ ILLUSTRATOR:

Randy Padorr-Black

PRINTER:

Lone Star Sportswear

DESIGN FIRM:

Alaska Serigraphics,

Anchorage, Alaska

ART DIRECTOR/

DESIGNER: David Powers

DESIGNER/ILLUSTRATOR:

Connie Hamedi

AGENCY: W.B. Doner, Troy, Michigan

ART DIRECTOR: Amy Swita

DESIGNER/ILLUSTRATOR: Stephen Schudlich

DESIGNER: Jeannine Caesar

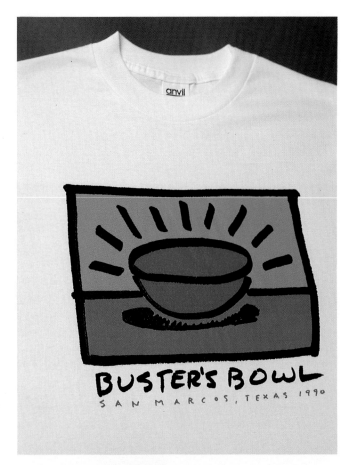

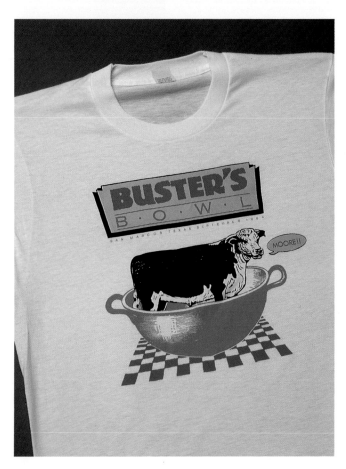

DESIGN FIRM:

Van Hayes Design, Dallas,

Texas

ART DIRECTOR/

DESIGNER/ ILLUSTRATOR:

Van Hayes

ILLUSTRATOR:

Brian Morren (Cowboy-

1986)

CLIENT: Buster Moore

Shirt for 9th cookoff and poster announcing 8th cookoff (below).

AGENCY:

The Beaird Agency, Dallas, Texas

DESIGN FIRM:

Zachow Design

ART DIRECTOR/

DESIGNER: Ed Zachow

ILLUSTRATOR: Paul Micich

CLIENT: The Chili Society Ltd.

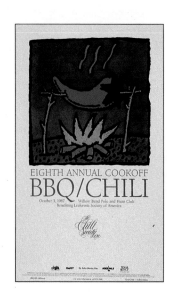

DESIGN FIRM:

Nike Apparel, Beaverton,

Oregon

ART DIRECTOR:

Angela Snow

DESIGNER: Randy Hamar

PHOTOGRAPHER:

Steve Wilkes (basketball

grafitti)

DESIGN FIRM:

McGuirk's Quirks,

Portsmouth,

New Hampshire

DESIGNER: Leslie McGuirk

SILKSCREENER:

Blue Point Design

DESIGN FIRM:

Dunn and Rice Design, Inc.,

Rochester, New York

ART DIRECTOR/

DESIGNER:

John Dunn

AIGA Rochester

DESIGN FIRM:

Dunn and Rice Design, Inc.,

Rochester, New York

ART DIRECTOR/

DESIGNER:

John Dunn

DESIGN FIRM:

Winterland Productions,

San Francisco, California

DESIGN FIRM/AGENCY:

Smith Novelty Co.

(shopping bag and hat)

DESIGNER:

Barbara Skurman/

Luke-A-Tuke

Barcelona Summer
Olympics promotion.

DESIGN FIRM:

Nike Art Department,

Beaverton, Oregon

ART DIRECTOR:

Angela Strike-Snow

DESIGNER:

West Armstrong

ILLUSTRATOR: Gary Evans

(sunburst)

PHOTOGRAPHER:

West Armstrong (runner

and Gaudi architecture)

DESIGN FIRM:

The Avrea Company,

Dallas, Texas

ART DIRECTOR/

DESIGNER/ ILLUSTRATOR:

Darren Avrea

Dockers' Modern Classic
clothing line.

DESIGN FIRM:

Sackett Design,

San Francisco, California

ART DIRECTOR/

DESIGNER/ COPYWRITER:

Mark Sackett

DESIGNER:

Wayne Sakamoto

(Expedition, Cranberry,

Modern Classic)

ILLUSTRATORS: Mark

Sackett, Wayne Sakamoto

(Gray, Navy, Blue, Global),

Chris Yaryan (Expedition,

Day or Night, Modern

Classic)

DESIGN FIRM:

Morreal Graphic Design,

San Diego, California

DESIGNER/ILLUSTRATOR:

Mary Lou Morreal

Event award (right).

DESIGN FIRM:

Padorr-Black Design

(1990), Dally Advertising

(1991), Arlington, Texas

ART DIRECTOR/

DESIGNER/ ILLUSTRATOR:

Randy Padorr-Black

PRINTER:

Silverwing Productions

CLIENT: Dallas YMCA

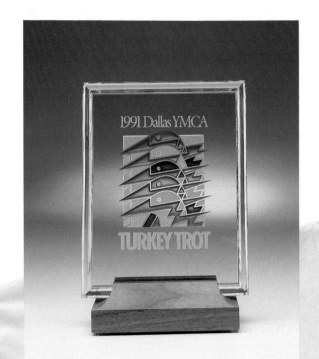

AGENCY:

Roberts & Olson

Advertising, Boston,

Massachusetts

DESIGNERS: Jon Olson,

Janet Palasek

FINISHED ART:

Michael Orzech

CLIENT:

Lifetime Corporation

DESIGN FIRM:

Cowell Design Group,

Burbank, California

ART DIRECTOR: Lee Cowell

DESIGNER: Kevin Weinman

PRINTING:

Characters & Color

Shirt commemorating

Mikhail Gorbachev's visit to

Minnesota.

DESIGN FIRM: Design Guys,

Minneapolis, Minnesota

ART DIRECTOR/

DESIGNER: Steven Sikora

DESIGNERS:

Lynette Sikora, Gary Patch

Annual Father's Day Fun Run

DESIGN FIRM:

Kornreich Gleason Design,

San Luis Obispo, California

ART DIRECTOR/

DESIGNER/ ILLUSTRATOR:

Catherine Kornreich

DESIGNER:

Melanie Gleason

CLIENT: KKUS Radio

Restaurant menu (right).

DESIGN FIRM: Promotion
Network, Arlington, Texas

ART DIRECTOR/

DESIGNER/ ILLUSTRATOR:

Gary Templin

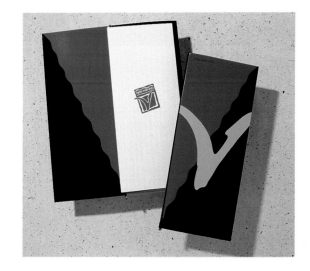

Viva Prima (Sportswear Collection)

Fabric design (far left),
workbook cover (left).

DESIGN FIRM:
Billings Quine Design
Group, Boulder, Colorado
ART DIRECTOR:
Susan Billings
DESIGNERS:
Nancy Miller-Hobbs
(workbook cover),
Susan Billings (T-shirt)
ILLUSTRATORS:
Nancy Miller-Hobbs
(T-shirt), Susan Billings
(fabric and T-shirt)
CLIENT: Prima Sports, Inc.

Nike

Shirt given to Nike-
sponsored athletes.

DESIGN FIRM: Nike Design,

Beaverton, Oregon

ART DIRECTOR:

Angela Snow

DESIGNER: Christine Redell

Stephen Schudlich Illustration & Design

Self-promotion collector

cards (right).

DESIGN FIRM:

Stephen Schudlich

Illustration & Design,

Troy, Michigan

ART DIRECTOR/

DESIGNER/ ILLUSTRATOR:

Stephen Schudlich

Skyscraper

Cake

Banana

Rocket

Strawberry

Shimokochi/Reeves Design

DESIGN FIRM:

Shimokochi/Reeves Design,

Los Angeles, California

ART DIRECTOR/

DESIGNER:

Mamoru Shimokochi

ART DIRECTOR/

DESIGNER: Anne Reeves

DESIGNER:

Tracy McGoldrick

AGENCY:

Ketchum Advertising/PHG,

Pittsburgh, Pennsylvania

ART DIRECTOR: Pati Ingold

COPYWRITER:

Sandy Stewart

Hogan's Market

DESIGN FIRM:

Hornall Anderson Design

Works, Seattle, Washington

ART DIRECTORS:

Jack Anderson, Julia LaPine

DESIGNERS: Julia LaPine,

Jack Anderson,

Denise Weir, Lian Ng

Bumper sticker (top right)
and mug (above) were used
as fund-raising premiums.
DESIGN FIRM:
DeLuise Design, Los
Angeles, California
ART DIRECTOR/
DESIGNER: Jim DeLuise

Annual Country Triathlon 1989

DESIGN FIRM:

Fritts & Hanna,

Erie, Pennsylvania

DESIGNERS/

ILLUSTRATORS:

Dawn Bishop, Ann Sluga

CLIENT:

St. Vincent Health Center

Holiday shirts.

DESIGN FIRM: Tilka Design,

Minneapolis, Minnesota

ART DIRECTOR/

DESIGNER/ ILLUSTRATOR:

Jane Tilka

Spike Lee product
promotion.
DESIGN FIRM: Nike Design,
Beaverton, Oregon
ART DIRECTOR:
Angela Snow
DESIGNER:
Sue K. Tackmier

DESIGN FIRM:

Design Promotion N.Y.,

New York, New York

ART DIRECTOR:

Patrick M. Sheeran

DESIGNER:

Deborah Winterson

CLIENT: Prudential Bache

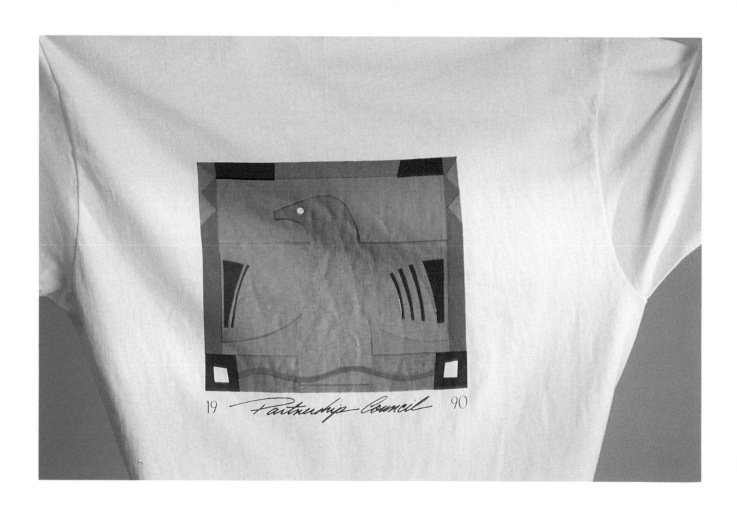

Danskin

DESIGN FIRM:

Design Promotion N.Y.,

New York, New York

ART DIRECTOR/

DESIGNER:

Patrick M. Sheeran

ILLUSTRATOR:

Bill Sweeney

DESIGN FIRM:

Kottler Caldera Group,

Phoenix, Arizona

ART DIRECTORS:

Dave Kottler, Paul Caldera,

Doreen Caldera

ART DIRECTOR/

DESIGNER/ ILLUSTRATOR:

Bart Welch

CLIENT: The New Times

Melons

Commemorating 75th birthday of Albert Schwenk, who raised melons on the plains of Nebraska all his life.

ART DIRECTOR/ DESIGNER: Ron Sack, Lincoln, Nebraska

COPYWRITER: Angela Bartels

CLIENT: Albert and Clara Schwenk

Postcard and invitation.

DESIGN FIRM:

Katz Wheeler Design,

Philadelphia, Pennsylvania

ART DIRECTOR/

DESIGNER: Joel Katz

DESIGNER: Alina Wheeler

DESIGN FIRM:

Venice T-shirt, Torrance,

California

ART DIRECTOR/

DESIGNER: Kathy Morton

DESIGN FIRM:

Mann Bukvic Associates,

Cincinnati, Ohio

CREATIVE DIRECTOR:

Dave Bukvic

ART DIRECTOR/

DESIGNER/ ILLUSTRATOR:

Cathy Bertke

DESIGN FIRM:

SHR Design

Communications,

Scottsdale, Arizona

ART DIRECTOR

DESIGNER/ ILLUSTRATOR:

Doug Reeder

Front.

DESIGN FIRM:

Boston College Office of

Communications, Chestnut

Hill, Massachusetts

ART DIRECTOR:

Jana Spacek

DESIGNER/ILLUSTRATOR:

Karen E. Roehr (red and

blue shirts)

DESIGNER/ILLUSTRATOR:

Monica DeSalvo

DESIGN FIRM:

Roger Chandler

Illustration/Design, La Jolla,

California

ART DIRECTOR/

DESIGNER/ ILLUSTRATOR:

Roger Chandler

HAWAII